BROKEN AND HEALED

HEAL FROM HEARTBREAK, STAY STRONG, MOVE ON, AND FIND LOVE AGAIN

Copyright ©2022 by Melissa Cory

No part of this publication may be reproduced, distributed, or transmitted in any form or by any means, including photocopying, recording, or other electronic or mechanical methods, without the prior written permission of the publisher, except in the case of brief quotations embodied in critical reviews and certain other noncommercial uses permitted by copyright law.

Images source: Unsplash.com

Table of Contents

CHAPTER ONE

This Is Love

You are the first and most valuable asset in a relationship. The other person comes next. However, the love you have for them makes you love them as you love yourself. You don't give them what you cannot accept yourself. This is how love works out and how you create a lasting relationship.

Love goes beyond what you stand to gain for yourself alone. Love is about what is good for everyone, not just for you or the other person. Some people think that true love is all about pleasing the other person only. No, it may seem so but, in essence, it is not. True love is about doing what is good for everyone involved in the relationship.

For instance, when you do the right thing, you help everyone in the relationship. You may not experience the benefit now, but you will notice it in your lives eventually.

In the same way, when you fail to do the right thing now, you hurt yourself and put the relationship at risk. In some cases, the future of the relationship becomes bleak. In the end, everyone suffers and loses abysmally.

Go as far as is right, proper, and decent to stay in love. If something is wrong now, it will be wrong in the future. If something will be wrong in the future, then it is wrong now. Sensible people always look at the future when making decisions. If something does not feel right now, it may never feel right later. If an attitude seems to harm the relationship now, then the damage may increase as time goes by. It is better to put an end to it and not let it get out of hand.

Ask yourself: "If I'm in the other person's shoes, is this the right thing to do? Would I like it? Would I be proud of this decision in the next five, ten or 20 years?" Once you have the answers, you solve almost all the problems that may arise in your relationship. This is the yardstick for measuring serious decisions or commitments.

ROMEO AND JULIET

The book *Romeo and Juliet* comes to mind. The sad end of the two youngsters makes one's heart tremble. Romeo and Juliet were in love with each other. Romeo loved Juliet, and Juliet loved Romeo. In the eyes of the public, they were the perfect partners. They would make the best couple and become a good example of true love.

At the beginning of the play, Romeo thought he was in love with Rosaline when he actually was in love with love itself. He was very young then and knew nothing of what true means. He was not ready to make the sacrifice needed to make a relationship work. Rosaline, too, was not helping matters in any way. She was full of herself and had neither the feeling nor the interest Romeo had.

Romeo's love for Rosaline consumed him, until the proud Rosaline broke up the relationship. Only then did

Romeo discover that he was only in love with love, not Rosaline. He had merely wanted to be like other young men in Venice. To trigger the chains of tragedy in the play, his two friends, the wise Benvolio and the clever Mercutio, advised Romeo to, "Examine other beauties."

That was the beginning of Romeo's tale of woes. However, the young Romeo learned true love the moment he set his eyes on Juliet. He found with her peace, love, acceptance, and sacrifice. The feelings between them were real, and these two lovers were willing to go the extra mile to make the relationship work. The eventual heartbreak didn't come from either of them. It came from the long hatred Romeo and Juliet's families had for each other.

Were it not for the hatred between the Montagues and the Capulets, their love would have blossomed into a beautiful lifelong relationship. The signs of a future heartbreak were there, but the two lovers chose to ignore them and paid the ultimate price. Reading their story always brings tears to one's eyes.

CHAPTER TWO

Do Good People exist?

A big difference exists between getting good things and getting good people in your life. Anybody can acquire good things, but not everybody can find good people. Good things may not bring good people, but good people can bring good things.

True happiness does not come from material possessions. Money and popularity may have their place, but they hardly guarantee a long and happy relationship. Love comes from the heart, and true love comes from the soul. True love is a deeper feeling than ordinary love. It creates a lasting bond with the significant other. This quality makes a couple begin to resemble each other. You can create this kind of bond with a good person.

People have asked the questions:

"Do good people exist?"

"Is it possible to be good?"

"How do I identify a good person?"

The answers to these questions are:

1. Good people exist.

2. It is possible to be good.

3. You can identify a good person as easily and quickly as you can identify yourself.

THE BIG CONFUSION

A big confusion we have in society today is that people who are supposed to be good are bad; people who are supposed to be bad are good.

Another shocking reality is that people who have both beauty and goodness are few in this world. You may easily get beauty and brain, but beauty and goodness are few and very scarce. As it is with women, so it is with men. Everyone seems to be guilty in this aspect. It's like a global pandemic.

Getting good people doesn't come easy. You may travel the whole world and not see them. You may search the internet and not find them. Being nice and courteous isn't the same as being good. There are stories of nice people, but one day something changed them and they became murderers.

HOW TO IDENTIFY GOOD PEOPLE

Only a good person knows what's good for everybody. If you are not a good person, you may never recognize another good person. Most people look for beauty, handsomeness, money, riches, or adventure. They do not search for or notice goodness when it passes by.

Good people are different. They don't do some things other people do. They do things other people don't do. If you can search them with this principle, you will easily find them wherever they are.

But listen! You may still never find good people until you become a good person. If it takes a thief to catch a thief, then it takes a good person to identify another good person. You have to work on yourself to attract good people.

Remember the law of attraction. No matter how you pretend to be good, you will attract people who behave like you. If you live in pretense, you cannot change whom you will attract. If you respect this law of attraction, you will have peace of mind and make fewer mistakes in your life choices.

Most people are quick to make decisions and draw a fixed conclusion. The idea of "You must accept me the way I am" is both archaic and unhelpful in any relationship. Think of it: if the other person takes you the way you are, can you accept the other person the way he or she is? To be accepted the way you are, you need to have the minimum good qualities, and then your imperfections will be accepted.

Millions of people are living in sadness and dissatisfaction today. The reason is that they want the world to pay attention to them. They care less about how others feel. They have no regard for anything that doesn't please them. Yet they want people to accept them the way they are.

TRULY SPECIAL

You should avoid this one wrong mindset. A wrong mindset gives you such a feeling that makes you think that other people do not have the same thing. This feeling can be deceptive and unreliable as it is good and pleasant.

What is this mindset or feeling? It is the feeling of being special. It is the mindset of "I am special, one-of-a-kind, a rare gem." This can make men and women think that they are too good or too important to accept the ordinary things of life. They fix their minds on an imaginary blissful future. They build castles in the air and patiently wait to reap where they did not sow.

The fact is that being special is relative. No one person is special everywhere and at every time. You may be special to someone but not special to another person. You may be special in one country but ordinary in another country. That is why you need to identify where and to who you are special.

This stark reality should keep us humble, sober, and wiser when we relate to people. Why? It is because this feeling of being special gives us false hope and makes us expect too much from our relationships. It is the reason for some of the heartbreaks we experience in relationships.

Imagine waking up every day to cuddle your partner, and stay glued to them all day. You don't want to let go of them. You want them to go nowhere but stay with you for a week or a month. You don't want them to see the outside world, not even to go to work. You feel that you are the only good and special thing they need in their lives. They don't need to make money or call family and friends. Your beauty, handsomeness, and love are all they need to survive throughout the relationship. Things don't work that way.

THE CHOICES YOU MAKE

When making a choice, avoid basing it on looks, ethnicity, education, royalty, riches, or material possessions. Make your choice based on values, good principles, vision, sense of direction, and other good qualities. However, in today's world, a level of education is vital for survival.

However, if those great values are found in ethnicity, education, or royalty, go for it. But have it at the back of your mind that you are responsible for every choice you make. Your right or wrong choice brought you where you are today. If the end of your story is pleasant, it means you made a good choice. If it's bitter, you had made a not-so-good choice. It is as simple as that, but it is better to make the right choice from the beginning.

No one is born to suffer and perish in that suffering. We are all born to come out of bad conditions. However, the choices we make determine how and where we end up. Life deals with us based on the contents of our hearts and the words of our mouths. Don't ever forget that. What you wish for will depend on who you are. You must make yourself worthy of the life you wish for.

Some people think that life owes them big time. While this is true in some areas, it has a dangerous side. People with this mindset feel that because they are tall, handsome, beautiful, or endowed, the world should bow at their feet. They prey on the hard work of others and see no need to work themselves. If you don't work to make something work, you lose everything. No matter how good-looking you are, try and add some value to your relationship. Don't leave everything in the hands of the other partner. It may empower them to manipulate the relationship the way they want. In some cases, they may choose to end the relationship, leaving you with a broken heart. No one deserves to have heartbreak. It is not a pleasant experience.

CHAPTER THREE

Healing from a Heartbreak I

When a relationship ends, the pain is often too much to handle. You discover that you had invested and depended so much on the relationship. Some people get over it by engaging in the other things they love.

Activities such as reading and watching movies may help some people go through the phase. Bouncing back becomes easy and they are ready to love again. Sometimes, the whole story ends in getting back your love or finding love with someone better. Whichever way, the healing process is what matters.

Unlike the things you see in movies, you cannot resolve relationship issues in a few hours. Movies are a snapshot of the longer periods of real life. While most storylines have happy conclusions, the case is usually not the same in the real world.

You may try to get over the heartbreak by repeating positive words and trying to focus your mind on a better future. Sometimes, these tricks are ineffective and only bring you back to where you were before the imaginary escape. While it is good to find encouragement from anyone and anything, not all solutions work out as expected. Everyone heals differently, and you will find yours eventually.

No matter how much friends and family love you, no one knows how long it takes to get over heartbreak. It is not as fast as getting out of an SUV. Relationships involve trust, sacrifice, and mutual plans. It takes time to unwind and take back your mind. It takes time to move from the path set out by the relationship. When people are in love, they make plans that will be of benefit to the relationship. When it is over, that path may no longer be the right one. This gets even tougher if the other partner is the brain behind the decision.

However, it is possible to heal from heartbreak, and proper healing takes time and personal effort. Do not worry about how long it may take. Focus on the process and allow it to

unwind and release you from the pain
and sorrow of the past.

BROKEN HEARTS CAN BE MENDED

One thing to keep in mind is that it is
not all over for you. A relationship
may end suddenly, sadly or
surprisingly, it doesn't matter how.
You may even get to know about
your failed relationship through a text
message, Instagram or WhatsApp.
Technology makes things more
complicated these days.

It's surprising how people go on
social media and announce the end of
a relationship that took months or
years to build. This indeed is weird.

However, if your relationship is over, try to put the past behind you and brace up for the journey towards healing.

WAYS TO HEAL YOUR BROKEN HEART

Do You First

The first person a breakup affects is you, not the other person. Remember that you got into the relationship in the first place because you loved it. It felt nice and you were okay with it. You thought that the other person was right for you. Now that it's over, you need to put your life back together. One of the things you may not notice is the gradual loss of appetite. You should never allow that to linger. In fact, it should be the first thing to watch out for and work on before it gets worse.

Emotional, spiritual, and mental aspects are also important. Try not to allow guilt, pain, anger, and stress to get the best of you. Consciously practice kindness and gentleness towards yourself and others. It is often natural to react in a negative way when you are hurting. Heartbreaks hurt deeply, and you may unconsciously overreact on some issues and make a mess of your relationship with other people. No matter what you go through, don't let it ruin what you feel for your family, friends, and you. Love yourself and maintain good personal hygiene. Don't let days go by without taking care of your hair or teeth.

Sometimes, it is best to look for a professional therapist who will walk through the healing process with you. It may sound great to keep your pains to yourself and not bother others with your sad tale. A skilled, trustworthy, and compassionate therapist can make a world of difference. What matters is getting you out of the woods as gradually as possible. It's never a good idea to be in a hurry to move on without first getting back your true self. Let someone knowledgeable guide you along the way. You may not be able to do it all alone. Be humble enough to admit it, and help will come your way naturally.

Practice Forgiveness

Sometimes, it is difficult to forgive the one who broke your heart. Some partners act as if they had no feelings for you in the first place. They just break the news and think you will be okay after that. The betrayal and pretense are so glaring that you want to hate them forever. Forgive them and work through the healing process. You have to understand that forgiving them doesn't mean you approve of their thoughtless deed.

Forgiveness sets you free to focus your attention and energy on important things. If the past is past and the relationship is over, then let forgiveness lead you out of the dark tunnel. You gain a lot emotionally and mentally when you forgive and forget how deeply you hurt. If the person or the situation doesn't worth the effort, then it isn't healthy to hinder your healing through a lack of forgiveness.

If you truly want to heal fast and move on quicker than you expect, you need to forgive the one person most affected by the failed relationship. That person is you, and you need to do it fast before you lose yourself to your pain. It is a lot easier to let go of your ex but extremely difficult to forgive yourself for being so silly to trust someone too soon. You may even recall some of the danger signs you ignored. You begin to wish you were wiser and had acted immediately you saw those indicators.

You cannot change what has happened. Work on changing yourself and evolving into a wiser and more knowledgeable person. Every human experience should teach one or two lessons. Relationships often leave behind tons of lessons. Learn from these mistakes and resolve in your heart never to allow them to repeat in your future relationships.

CHAPTER FOUR

Healing from a
Heartbreak II

Love the Good Old Days

Relationships, no matter how badly they end, have some good memories to cherish. Some relationships began fine but later turned sour. Others were shaky from the start and fell apart suddenly. Despite how awful you feel and how much you want to get the thoughts off your mind, you still have some golden moments to cherish. Your ex has some sides that make you smile and laugh. Those memories kept you moving when you noticed the gradual decline of the bond you shared. Now that it is all over between you two, try to appreciate those times. Let them be the only things you could take out of the failed relationship.

Even sour fruits have their own type of sweetness when you view them with fresh eyes. Look back to those wonderful days and recall the moments that thrilled your heart so much that you wished they repeated themselves. It may a funny photo pose or the first time your ex taught you scuba diving. It could be anything.

Not everyone has those amazing moments. You should be grateful that you do. Try not to dismiss everything as a failure. Don't let in resentment or they will make you unaware of how happy you were in the past relationship. Ride out the emotional shifts and give room for healing. You gain a lot when you show enough gratitude for the smallest things in life. And a relationship is no small matter.

Don't Rush

Some people believe that the solution to a failed relationship is to find love immediately. It sounds logical to think that when love breaks a heart, only love can mend it. While this may sound true, it's not advisable to jump into another relationship before healing properly. A newly found love will deprive you of the lessons from the past one. If you don't take time to reflect and learn from what happened in the past relationship, you may not cope well in the new one.

You may repeat the same mistake if you don't learn from the breakup. People don't often appear to be who they make you believe they are. You need time and quiet moments to heal and begin to use your head properly again. Get the cobwebs off your brain and put that brain into use so no one breaks your heart again in the future.

Jump In When Ready

People who were in long-term relationships usually take more time to heal. The long period of time they spent with each other makes it difficult to move on. However, a breakup and heartbreak don't mean the end of the world. You were you when you entered into the relationship and you are still you now. You are who you are and no one has the right to take away who you are. Spending time on your own for the first time in a long while has its own advantages. You find the opportunity to think about your life and put your focus back on yourself.

Since the other partner is no longer in your life, you are free to redefine your values. This may be a bit difficult if you lived to look after others. The difficulty increases when you are antisocial and comfortable in a social gathering only when you are with your partner. Others may not mind being in the public eye after the worst heartbreak just to get their minds off their worries. Everyone has their own individual differences.

It is fine if you don't feel like going out again. The fear of seeing the lost partner can trigger unwanted feelings. Seeing your ex may even do more harm if you cross paths. Sometimes you come across someone you know who would try to ask about your ex and how both of you are doing. You don't want to tell a lie, so you avoid going outside at all.

Every useful decision you make is good and may help to speed up the healing process. Try not to go extreme with your isolation. You don't have a contagious virus. You only had heartbreak and it is not the end of your life or happiness. You still have a beautiful and amazing future waiting for you. Find a friend who understands your mood and who can respect your boundary. Let that one person stay with you or tag along as you visit the church, favorite sports team, library, or any place you feel like going.

Fix Your Emotions

A broken relationship or divorce doesn't make you a failure. You are not a failure and you will not be one. Don't spend time thinking about how you failed and couldn't handle a relationship. Even if it is your first, see it as a period of learning and growing in knowledge and wisdom. You didn't know some of the things you know now. If you knew them, you would have seen the heartbreak coming and avoided it.

Breakups help you to know yourself better. Use those things you discovered to work on yourself. Make yourself better and choose to emerge stronger and bigger than your former self. Anger may lurk somewhere in your heart. Don't let it rule your life. Don't let it push you to embark on a payback journey. Don't even think of ruining your former partner's life or making them never find love again. If the other person has moved on, don't put a stumbling block in their way.

Your pain doesn't grow less when you hurt others and give them a taste of their own pudding. Your pain is in your heart and mind and there is no way you can transfer it. In fact, you may likely feel worse after the whole drama. In addition, you slow down your healing process when you try to get even with your ex.

Let Go of the Past

Looking back on the past is one major mistake you should try to avoid as much as you can. Going back and thinking of the worst moments will do you no good. Sometimes, it is tough to get the endless stream of bad thoughts out of your mind. You keep playing them repeatedly in your mind, looking at the meanings of every moment you shared. This interfering thought can stall the healing process. They can cause you much distress.

While it is difficult to let go of some parts of the past, stay focused on getting out of the dark hole. No one is perfect, and no relationship is perfect. Seeing yours as perfect makes it too hard to bear when it is all over. If you have felt like your ex was the best thing that ever happened to you, you make a mistake. No one is perfect and neither is your ex.

Avoid regular habits that may keep the pain fresh. Practices such as viewing their social media activities can trigger the pain or make you lose your mind. In the digital age, it takes many efforts to block the mind from social media content begging for attention. Facebook, Twitter, and Instagram use clever ways to lure users into checking what other people are doing. You could go crazy if you stumble on the photo of your ex with a new lover. The internet and social media do not always understand the emotional implications of what they show us. So, keep some physical distance if you must heal well and move on in a short time.

Simple Tips on How to Let Go of the Past

1. Determine to let go.

1. Accept responsibility for the breakup that led to the heartbreak.

2. Live in the present moment only.

3. Be kind to yourself.

4. Reduce triggers and reminders of your past relationship.

5. Set your boundary and respect them.

6. Stop every form of contact with your ex.

7. Spend time working on yourself.

8. Write down how you feel and then throw the paper away.

9. Play music that expresses how you feel inside without triggering your unwanted emotions.

10. Forgive the other person sincerely.

11. Don't feel entitled to the other person's love and attention.

12. Accept that it is normal to feel sad.

13. Identify what stops you from moving on with your life.

14. Think of what you can change for the future.

15. Ask for professional help when needed.

16. Confide in someone you trust.

17. Exercise every day for at least 20 minutes.

18. Spend time with the right people.

19. Take up hobbies that you are most passionate about.

20. Never spend too much time alone except when you sleep.

CHAPTER FIVE

Healing from a Heartbreak III

Reevaluate Your Choices

Your choice of partner may be the reason for the heartbreak. You might have been careful. The problem could be that you did not consider your exact needs before going into that relationship. It is true that you have needs and want those needs met. It can be painful when those needs are unmet and you have to live each day seeking satisfaction.

The truth is that your previous relationship couldn't meet those needs. If it did, you wouldn't be talking about breakup or heartbreak now. So, reconcile with the fact that the failed relationship was not able to give you enough satisfaction. Now use the healing process to think of the qualities you truly need in a partner. Only someone with most or all of those qualities can stay with you longer and satisfy you better. Anything short of what you need may end up in heartbreak. Be blunt with the truth and choose to make a better choice next time.

Twenty Questions to Help Reevaluate Your Relationship

1. Do you have frequent arguments?

2. Do you hear each other out or yell at each other?

3. Do you resolve issues based on the needs of everyone involved?

4. How do you make important decisions?

5. Who makes the decisions in the relationship?

6. Do you have plans?

7. Are these plans worth the trouble?

8. How much of your dreams do you share with each other?

9. Does your partner show interest in your dreams?

10. Are you compatible or do you notice large areas of incompatibility?

11. Is the other person emotionally available?

12. Are you always yourself when together with your partner?

13. Do you share the same values for work and relationships?

14. Does each of you demand different things from each other?

15. Do you feel that something has gone wrong even when no words are spoken?

16. Do you naturally play with your partner or always have to create the time?

17. Does the play feel great or forced and mechanical?

18. Do you have absolute trust in your partner?

19. What areas do you have some doubts about them?

20. Can you count on the other person in times of emergencies?

Take Time to Grieve

There is no shame in crying and grieving. Strong people cry, so why won't you? Breakups hurt and it takes time to forget all the great moments you had with your ex. Take time to grieve, and don't rush it. Allow the tears to flow and don't try to stop even a drop of tear. Stilling your emotion and pretending to be superhuman will have a negative psychological effect on you.

Accept the feeling of sadness and pain and allow it to do its cleansing work. You may choose to be alone. That's fine, so far you are in control. If there are tendencies to harm yourself, have a friend stay with you. Healing time helps you take inventory of your life, the patterns you followed, and the choice you made. Allow this important moment to take you into the nature of your inner self, desires, and needs.

How to Grieve a Breakup

1. Allow anger and sadness to flow out.

2. Learn to do things alone.

3. Go for things that you love.

4. Identify what you feel at the thought of your ex.

5. Tell others how you feel.

6. Keep in mind that you have to move on at the end of it all.

7. Always remember that you still have a wonderful future.

8. Step out occasionally.

9. Make new and understanding friends.

10. Stick to a useful daily routine.

11. Stay away from drugs, alcohol, and overeating.

12. Find new areas of interest.

13. Stay in touch with family members.

14. Avoid reaching out to your ex.

15. Don't go into a new relationship.

16. Eat healthy foods.

17. Create time for uninterrupted sleep.

18. Watch out for the feeling of hopelessness and helplessness.

19. Let go of resentment and hatred for your ex.

20. Stay in control of your life.

Move About

The very first thing that could come to you is the idea that sitting or sleeping all day would help in dealing with a breakup. While this comes naturally, it is not the right thing to do, as the body needs to move about freely without being confined to a specific place. Do not allow yourself to be trapped in this bad habit while trying to heal your heart.

Exercise will help you avoid the negative feelings that come to the brokenhearted. Do some workouts such as walking, biking, running, or jogging. You can incorporate online exercises into your daily routine just to keep out the lack of movement. A sedentary lifestyle is a breeding ground for unwanted feelings such as stress, sadness, lethargy, and anxiety. Keep these feelings out as much as you can as you make progress in your healing journey.

CHAPTER SIX

Healing from a
Heartbreak IV

Think About Other People

A broken heart rarely recognizes the days of the week or the faces of people. Each day looks the same and each day comes with the same boring routines of daily living. It takes time and effort to take notice of family and friends around you. Do not allow your grief to overwhelm you so much that you do not care for the feelings and needs of the people in your life. These people may be your elderly parents, your kids, your coworkers, or friends and neighbors. Your grieving moment is the best time you need them most.

Create some time to have a chat with them. Walk around and spare a minute or two for them. When you focus your attention on the needs of others, it helps to get your mind off your worries. This is a useful distraction, as you work towards the healing process. You may consider working as a volunteer in a local book club, animal shelter, or soup kitchen. Alternatively, you can help a friend or neighbor prepare meals, mow the lawn or do spring cleaning. Anything to give your thoughts enough space to allow for inner healing is welcome.

What to Do to Help Other People

1. Use kind words whenever you speak or act.
2. Give them your time.

3. Teach at a local school as a volunteer.

4. Join a food bank.

5. Work with a retirement home.

6. Volunteer at an animal shelter.

7. Give out unused items to those who need them.

8. Learn to say "Thank You."

9. Help at a charity home.

10. Carry the grocery for an elderly person.

11. Stop to help someone fix a flat tire.

12. Be the friend of a grieving person.

13. Help people make the right decisions.

14. Encourage others to take action.

15. Give listening ears to those in trouble.

16. Show kindness to the homeless and hungry.

17. Help somebody to kick out laziness and procrastination.

18. Send a text message or email to family and friends every week.

19. Be there for someone.

20. Stand with the voiceless.

21. Volunteer to babysit a neighbor's baby.

22. Share the little knowledge you have.

23. Make people aware of opportunities they could miss.

24. Be a counselor to someone.

25. Motivate others to work hard and be smart.

26. Give someone a sense of purpose and direction.

27. Help someone do shopping.

28. Help a coworker buy lunch.

29. Ask to take a neighbor's pet out for a walk.

30. Practice random acts of kindness.

Make Positive Confessions

Negative feelings often come uninvited when you are down. Fight them with everything you got. However, a way to curb these is to find something you love about yourself. Think of the amazing things you can do, like wash clothes until they sparkle, iron dresses until they look like navy uniforms, or speak like some of the best orators the world has ever known. If you take the time to practice this, you will be amazed at how many things you are good at. Take your time to write them down and confess to yourself that you are good enough.

Another thing to do is make positive confessions. You may write them down to help you recite them every morning, afternoon, and evening. Say them whenever you feel like giving in to negative emotions. Positive confessions actually work if you do them right. Give them all the inner and outer concentration you got, and believe every word you say.

Sample of Positive Confessions to Help You Through the Healing Process

1. I am not a failure. I am a successful person.

2. I have all the confidence I need to learn and grow.

3. I am emotionally and mentally strong to go through this phase of my life.

4. Everything I need is within me at this moment.

5. I am motivated to live a happy and fulfilled every day.

6. I am unstoppable and powerful.

7. I am getting better in character, attitude, and behavior every day.

8. My past does not define me. My future is what matters.

9. I am self-sufficient and can do things on my own.

10. No obstacle can stand in my way. I am victorious.

11. I am so grateful for life and everything I have right now.

12. Nothing can stop me from becoming whatever I want to be.

13. I will be highly productive today.

14. I am amazing, smart, and focused.

15. I free myself from all negative feelings and thoughts.

16. I accept who I am and what I can do.

17. I welcome peace, joy, and happiness into my mind, heart, and life.

18. I forgive the people who wronged me.

19. I forgive myself and free my mind from every confinement and limitation.

20. I believe that inner healing is taking place right now.

21. No single day of my life will be wasted.

22. I possess the incredible power to accomplish anything.

23. I am not other people, and other people are not me. I am unique and talented.

24. I am so proud of who and what I will become.

25. I let go of the limiting part of my past and I move on to better things.

26. This is my time to shine like the morning star.

27. I live with purpose and meaning.

28. I choose to be happy and fulfilled.

29. I am strong and smart enough to make personal decisions
   a. .

30. I can love and will love again.

31. I am in charge of what I do and say.

32. I love everything about myself.

33. I have a healthy body and mind.

34. My happiness doesn't depend on other people.

35. I do not criticize myself for my past mistakes and wrong choices.

36. I possess the limitless potential to succeed.

37. I choose to learn from my mistakes, not fall under them.

38. I do my best and that is enough for me.

39. I do not live my life on the internet. I have the real me right here with me.

40. I have everything to attract respect and acceptance everywhere I go.

41. I have a lot to contribute to other people and to the world.

42. I open my heart and mind to a fresh start and new adventures.

43. I love my body the way it is.

44. I kick out worry and anxiety.

45. I choose to see the best part of me in everything.

46. I have no need for people's approval or applause.

47. I move forward in all areas of life.

48. My happiness and peace are my responsibility.

49. I am grateful for each day.

50. I possess resilience and the ability to handle anything.

For the religious or spiritual person, prayer, meditation and attending religious gathering is an added advantage. You may also choose to see your spiritual leader, pastor, imam or reverend for deep discussions on how you are dealing with the matters of the heart.

Overcoming heartbreak is one of the hardest thing in the world. It is painful and can cause you a lot of physical and psychological discomfort. But it is not impossible to win the battle. If you are heart is broke and you don't know what to do, the solutions proffered in this book will go a long way to bring you relief and healing. They are practical and helpful to anyone who is currently experiencing heartbreak and wants to come out of it.

Here is a summary of all the things to do to heal from heartbreak

1. Think about you first and take care of your body and mind every way you can.

2. Forgive your ex and forgive yourself too.

3. Cherish those wonderful moments you had together even when they are few.

4. Don't rush into another relationship thinking that it will heal your heart faster.

5. When you are ready, find true love in another person better and more caring than your ex.

6. Get rid of anger and resentment and learn from the breakup and heartbreak.

7. Forget the past hurt and think of a way to move forward.

8. Reevaluate your needs, desires and expectations in relationships.

9. Allow enough time to grieve, and don't try to stop your grief.

10. Don't sit or sleep all day. Try and move about to avoid more physical or psychological harm.

11. Create time for other people and help them the best way you can.

12. Make positive confessions and believe them with all of your heart.

You will be alright at the end of it all.
Believe it.

www.ingramcontent.com/pod-product-compliance
Lightning Source LLC
Chambersburg PA
CBHW061709130726
47996CB00006B/2232